The Thinking Tree

PONDERING THE PAST
AN INTRODUCTION TO
30 CLASSICAL STORIES

30 Fascinating Examples of
Classical English Literature
and Famous Authors
Focusing on the Years
1719 to 1912

ILLUSTRATIONS BY: HALEY REUST
COMPILED BY KATYA BRETUSH

Designed by Alexandra Bretush
Project Managed By: Sarah Janisse Brown

Open Dyslexic Font

The Thinking Tree, LLC

TABLE OF CONTENTS:

I. ROBINSON CRUSOE

Genre: Historical Fiction; Adventure Novel
Author: Daniel Defoe
Published: 1719

Daniel Defoe (1660 – April 24, 1731), born Daniel Foe, was an English trader, writer, journalist, pamphleteer, and spy, but he was most famous for his novel Robinson Crusoe. He was a prolific and versatile writer, producing more than five hundred books, pamphlets, and journals on various topics, including politics, crime, religion, marriage, psychology, and the supernatural. The most popular of his novels are *Robinson Crusoe*, *Captain Singleton*, *A Journal of the Plague Year*, *Colonel Jack*, and *Moll Flanders*.

CHAPTER 15 - FRIDAY'S EDUCATION

I described to him the country of Europe, particularly England, which I came from; how we lived, how we worshipped God, how we behaved to one another, and how we traded in ships to all parts of the world. I gave him an account of the wreck which I had been on board of and showed him, as near as I could, the place where she lay; but she was all beaten in pieces before and gone. I showed him the ruins of our boat, which we lost when we escaped, and which I could not stir with my whole strength then; but was now fallen almost all to pieces. Upon seeing this boat, Friday stood, musing a great while and said nothing. I asked him what it was he studied upon. At last says he, "Me see such boat like come to place at my nation." I did not understand him a good while; but at last, when I had examined further into it, I understood by him that a boat, such as that had been, came on shore upon the country where he lived. That it, as he explained it, was driven thither by stress of weather. I presently imagined that some European ship must have been cast away upon their coast, and the boat might get loose and drive ashore; but was so dull that I never once thought of men making their escape from a wreck thither, much less whence they might come: so I only inquired after a description of the boat.

VOCABULARY QUEST

Highlight and define two interesting or unfamiliar words.

Use a dictionary to explore the meaning of each word.

1._____

_____

2._____

_____

CLASSICAL COPYWORK

Copy two paragraphs from any book by this author

Title: _____

Author: _____

Time and Place of Publishing: _____

Names & descriptions of characters:

_____
_____
_____
_____
_____

Copy two paragraphs here:

_____
_____
_____
_____
_____
_____
_____
_____
_____
_____
_____
_____
_____
_____
_____
_____
_____
_____
_____

CREATE AN ILLUSTRATION

Make sure your artwork reflects the situation
in the selection of literature you use for your copywork.

WHAT CAN YOU LEARN ABOUT THE PAST FROM THIS STORY?

2. GULLIVER'S TRAVELS (Travels into several remote nations of the world. In four parts. By Lemuel Gulliver, first a surgeon and then a captain of several ships)

Genre: Satire; Parody

Author: Jonathan Swift.

Written: 1726 (Amended in 1735)

Jonathan Swift (November 30, 1667 – October 19, 1745) was an Anglo-Irish satirist, essayist, political pamphleteer, poet, and clergyman. Swift is remembered for works such as *Gulliver's Travels*, *A Modest Proposal*, *A Journal to Stella*, *The Battle of the Books*, and *A Tale of a Tub*. He is regarded as the foremost prose satirist in the English language. His ironic writing style has led to such satire being subsequently termed "Swiftian."

PART 1 – A VOUAGE TO LILLIPUT

CHAPTER 6

[Of the inhabitants of Lilliput; their learning, laws, and customs; the manner of educating their children. The author's way of living in that country. His vindication of a great lady.]

I shall say, but little at present of their learning, which, for many ages, has flourished in all its branches among them. Their manner of writing is very peculiar, being neither from the left to the right, like the Europeans, nor from the right to the left, like the Arabians, nor from up to down, like the Chinese, but aslant, from one corner of the paper to the other, like ladies in England.

They bury their dead with their heads directly downward, because they hold an opinion that in eleven thousand moons they are all to rise again. They believe the earth, which they conceive to be flat, will turn upside down, and by this means they shall, at their resurrection, be found ready standing on their feet. The learned among them confess the absurdity of this doctrine, but the practice still continues, in compliance to the vulgar.

There are some laws and customs in this empire that are very peculiar and if they were not so directly contrary to those of my own dear country, I would be tempted to say a little in their justification. It is only to be wished that they were as well executed. The first I shall mention, relates to informers. All crimes against the state are punished here with the utmost severity, but if the person accused makes his innocence plainly to appear upon his trial, the accuser is immediately put to an ignominious death. Out of his goods or lands, the innocent person is quadruply recompensed for the loss of his time, for the danger he underwent, for the hardship of his imprisonment and for all the charges he has incurred in making his defence. If that fund be deficient, it is largely supplied by the crown. The emperor also confers on him some public mark of his favour, and proclamation is made of his innocence through the whole city.

CLASSICAL COPYWORK

Copy two paragraphs from any book by this author

Title: _____

Author: _____

Time and Place of Publishing: _____

Names & descriptions of characters:

_____
_____
_____
_____
_____

Copy two paragraphs here:

_____
_____
_____
_____
_____
_____
_____
_____
_____
_____
_____
_____
_____
_____
_____
_____
_____
_____
_____
_____

CREATE AN ILLUSTRATION

Make sure your artwork reflects the situation
in the selection of literature you use for your copywork.

WHAT CAN YOU LEARN ABOUT THE PAST FROM THIS STORY?

3. PRIDE AND PREJUDICE

Genre: Novel of Manners; Satire

Author: Jane Austen

Published: 1813

Jane Austen (December 16, 1775 – July 18, 1817) was the most famous woman novelist in English and world literature, known principally for her five major novels which interpret, critique, and comment upon the life of the British landed gentry at the end of the 18th century. Austen's main novels, *Sense and Sensibility* (1811), *Pride and Prejudice* (1813), *Mansfield Park* (1814), *Emma* (1815), *Northanger Abbey* (1818), and *Persuasion* (1818), are rarely out of print today. Although, they were first published anonymously and brought her little personal fame with only a few glancing reviews during her lifetime.

CHAPTER 19

"You must give me leave to flatter myself, my dear cousin, that your refusal of my addresses is merely words of course. My reasons for believing it are briefly these: It does not appear to me that my hand is unworthy of your acceptance, or that the establishment I can offer would be any other than highly desirable. My situation in life, my connections with the family of de Bourgh, and my relationship to your own, are circumstances highly in my favour; and you should take it into further consideration, that in spite of your manifold attractions, it is by no means certain that another offer of marriage may ever be made you. Your portion is unhappily so small that it will in all likelihood undo the effects of your loveliness and amiable qualifications. As I must therefore conclude that you are not serious in your rejection of me, I shall choose to attribute it to your wish of increasing my love by suspense, according to the usual practice of elegant females."

VOCABULARY QUEST

Highlight and define three interesting or unfamiliar words.

Use a dictionary to explore the meaning of each word.

1. _____

_____

2. _____

_____

3. _____

_____

CLASSICAL COPYWORK

Copy two paragraphs from any book by this author

Title:_____

Author:_____

Time and Place of Publishing:_____

Names & descriptions of characters:

_____
_____
_____
_____
_____
_____

Copy two paragraphs here:

_____
_____
_____
_____
_____
_____
_____
_____
_____
_____
_____
_____
_____
_____
_____
_____
_____
_____
_____
_____
_____
_____

CREATE AN ILLUSTRATION

Make sure your artwork reflects the situation
in the selection of literature you use for your copywork.

WHAT CAN YOU LEARN ABOUT THE PAST FROM THIS STORY?

4. EMMA

Genre: Novel of Manners

Author: Jane Austen

Published: 1815

Jane Austen (December 16, 1775 – July 18, 1817) was the most famous woman novelist in English and world literature, known principally for her five major novels which interpret, critique and comment upon the life of the British landed gentry at the end of the 18th century. Austen's main novels, *Sense and Sensibility* (1811), *Pride and Prejudice* (1813), *Mansfield Park* (1814), *Emma* (1815), *Northanger Abbey* (1818), and *Persuasion* (1818), are rarely out of print today. Although, they were first published anonymously and brought her little personal fame with only a few glancing reviews during her lifetime.

VOLUME 1 CHAPTER 3

Mr. Woodhouse was fond of society in his own way. He liked very much to have his friends come and see him; and from various united causes, from his long residence at Hartfield, and his good nature, from his fortune, his house, and his daughter, he could command the visits of his own little circle, in a great measure, as he liked. He had not much intercourse with any families beyond that circle; his horror of late hours and large dinner-parties made him unfit for any acquaintance, but such as would visit him on his own terms. Fortunately for him, Highbury, including Randalls in the same parish, and Donwell Abbey in the parish adjoining, the seat of Mr. Knightley, comprehended many such. Not unfrequently, through Emma's persuasion, he had some of the chosen and the best to dine with him, but evening-parties were what he preferred, and, unless he fancied himself at any time unequal to company, there was scarcely an evening in the week in which Emma could not make up a card-table for him.

Real, long-standing regard brought the Westons and Mr. Knightley; and by Mr. Elton, a young man living alone without liking it, the privilege of exchanging any vacant evening of his own blank solitude for the elegancies and society of Mr. Woodhouse's drawing-room and the smiles of his lovely daughter, was in no danger of being thrown away.

VOCABULARY QUEST

Highlight and define two interesting or unfamiliar words.

Use a dictionary to explore the meaning of each word.

1._____

_____

2._____

_____

CLASSICAL COPYWORK

Copy two paragraphs from any book by this author

Title: _____

Author: _____

Time and Place of Publishing: _____

Names & descriptions of characters:

_____
_____
_____
_____
_____
_____

Copy two paragraphs here:

_____
_____
_____
_____
_____
_____
_____
_____
_____
_____
_____
_____
_____
_____
_____
_____
_____
_____
_____
_____

CREATE AN ILLUSTRATION

Make sure your artwork reflects the situation
in the selection of literature you use for your copywork.

WHAT CAN YOU LEARN ABOUT THE PAST FROM THIS STORY?

5. IVANHOE

Genre: Historical Novel

Author: Sir Walter Scott

Published: 1820

Sir Walter Scott, 1st Baronet, (August 15, 1771 – September 21, 1832) was a Scottish historical novelist, playwright, and poet with many contemporary readers in Europe, Australia, and North America.

Scott's novels and poetry are still read, and many of his works remain classics of both English-language literature and of Scottish literature. Famous titles include *Ivanhoe*, *Rob Roy*, *Old Mortality*, *The Lady of the Lake*, *Waverley*, *The Heart of Midlothian*, and *The Bride of Lammermoor*.

Although primarily remembered for his extensive literary works and his political engagement, Scott was an advocate, judge, and legal administrator by profession. Throughout his career, he combined his writing and editing work with his daily occupation as Clerk of Session and Sheriff-Depute of Selkirkshire.

CHAPTER 12

According to due formality, the Disinherited Knight was to be considered as leader of the one body, while Brian de Bois-Guilbert, who had been rated as having done second-best in the preceding day, was named first champion of the other band. Those who had concurred in the challenge adhered to his party of course, excepting only Ralph de Vipont, whom his fall had rendered unfit so soon to put on his armour. There was no want of distinguished and noble candidates to fill up the ranks on either side.

In fact, although the general tournament, in which all knights fought at once, was more dangerous than single encounters, they were, nevertheless, more frequented and practised by the chivalry of the age. Many knights, who had not sufficient confidence in their own skill to defy a single adversary of high reputation, were, nevertheless, desirous of displaying their valour in the general combat, where they might meet others with whom they were more upon an equality. On the present occasion, about fifty knights were inscribed as desirous of combating upon each side, when the marshals declared that no more could be admitted, to the disappointment of several who were too late in preferring their claim to be included.

About the hour of ten o'clock, the whole plain was crowded with horsemen, horsewomen, and foot-passengers, hastening to the tournament; and shortly after, a grand flourish of trumpets announced Prince John and his retinue, attended by many of those knights who meant to take share in the game, as well as others who had no such intention.

CLASSICAL COPYWORK

Copy two paragraphs from any book by this author

Title: _____

Author: _____

Time and Place of Publishing: _____

Names & descriptions of characters:

_____
_____
_____
_____
_____
_____

Copy two paragraphs here:

_____
_____
_____
_____
_____
_____
_____
_____
_____
_____
_____
_____
_____
_____
_____
_____
_____
_____
_____
_____

CREATE AN ILLUSTRATION

Make sure your artwork reflects the situation
in the selection of literature you use for your copywork.

WHAT CAN YOU LEARN ABOUT THE PAST FROM THIS STORY?

6. THE PICKWICK PAPERS

(The Posthumous Papers of the Pickwick Club)

Genre: Novel

Author: Charles Dickens

Published: 1836

Charles John Huffam Dickens (February 7, 1812 – June 9, 1870) was an English writer and social critic. He is one of the most popular storytellers of all time. He created some of the world's best-known fictional characters and is regarded as the greatest novelist of the Victorian era. Dickens published more than a dozen major novels, a large number of short stories, including a number of Christmas-themed stories, a handful of plays, and several non-fiction books. Among them are *The Posthumous Papers of the Pickwick Club, The Adventures of Oliver Twist, A Christmas Carol, David Copperfield, Little Dorrit, A Tale of Two Cities,* and *Our Mutual Friend.*

CHAPTER 12 – DESCRIPTIVE OF A VERY IMPORTANT PROCEEDING

Mr. Pickwick's apartments in Goswell Street, although on a limited scale, were not only of a very neat and comfortable description, but peculiarly adapted for the residence of a man of his genius and observation. His sitting-room was the first-floor front, his bedroom the second-floor front; and thus, whether he were sitting at his desk in his parlour, or standing before the dressing-glass in his dormitory, he had an equal opportunity of contemplating human nature in all the numerous phases it exhibits, in that not more populous than popular thoroughfare. His landlady, Mrs. Bardell—the relict and sole executrix of a deceased custom-house officer—was a comely woman of bustling manners and agreeable appearance, with a natural genius for cooking, improved by study and long practice, into an exquisite talent. There were no children, no servants, no fowls. The only other inmates of the house were a large man and a small boy; the first a lodger, the second a production of Mrs. Bardell's. The large man was always home precisely at ten o'clock at night, at which hour he regularly condensed himself into the limits of a dwarfish French bedstead in the back parlour; and the infantine sports and gymnastic exercises of Master Bardell were exclusively confined to the neighbouring pavements and gutters. Cleanliness and quiet reigned throughout the house; and in it Mr. Pickwick's will was law.

VOCABULARY QUEST

Highlight and define one interesting or unfamiliar word.

Use a dictionary to explore the meaning of the word.

1. _____

_____

CLASSICAL COPYWORK

Copy two paragraphs from any book by this author

Title: _____

Author: _____

Time and Place of Publishing: _____

Names & descriptions of characters:

_____
_____
_____
_____
_____

Copy two paragraphs here:

_____
_____
_____
_____
_____
_____
_____
_____
_____
_____
_____
_____
_____
_____
_____
_____
_____
_____
_____
_____
_____

CREATE AN ILLUSTRATION

Make sure your artwork reflects the situation
in the selection of literature you use for your copywork.

WHAT CAN YOU LEARN ABOUT THE PAST FROM THIS STORY?

7. OLIVER TWIST

(The Parish Boy's Progress)
Genre: Novel
Author: Charles Dickens
Published: 1837–39 (serialized) and 1838 (in book form)

Charles John Huffam Dickens (February 7, 1812 – June 9, 1870) was an English writer and social critic. He is one of the most popular storytellers of all time. He created some of the world's best-known fictional characters and is regarded as the greatest novelist of the Victorian era. Dickens published more than a dozen major novels, a large number of short stories, including a number of Christmas-themed stories, a handful of plays, and several non-fiction books. Among them are *The Posthumous Papers of the Pickwick Club*, *The Adventures of Oliver Twist*, *A Christmas Carol*, *David Copperfield*, *Little Dorrit*, *A Tale of Two Cities*, and *Our Mutual Friend*.

CHAPTER 10

Although Oliver had been brought up by philosophers, he was not theoretically acquainted with the beautiful axiom that self-preservation is the first law of nature. If he had been, perhaps he would have been prepared for this. Not being prepared, however, it alarmed him the more; so away he went like the wind, with the old gentleman and the two boys roaring and shouting behind him.

"Stop thief! Stop thief!" There is a magic in the sound. The tradesman leaves his counter, and the carman his waggon; the butcher throws down his tray; the baker his basket; the milkman his pail; the errand-boy his parcels; the school-boy his marbles; the paviour his pick-axe; the child his battledore. Away they run, pell-mell, helter-skelter, slap-dash: tearing, yelling, screaming, knocking down the passengers as they turn the corners, rousing up the dogs, and astonishing the fowls: and streets, squares, and courts, re-echo with the sound.

"Stop thief! Stop thief!" *The cry is taken up by a hundred voices, and the crowd accumulate at every turning. Away they fly, splashing through the mud, and rattling along the pavements: up go the windows, out run the people, onward bear the mob, a whole audience desert Punch in the very thickest of the plot, and, joining the rushing throng.*

CLASSICAL COPYWORK

Copy two paragraphs from any book by this author

Title: _____

Author: _____

Time and Place of Publishing: _____

Names & descriptions of characters:

_____
_____
_____
_____
_____

Copy two paragraphs here:

_____
_____
_____
_____
_____
_____
_____
_____
_____
_____
_____
_____
_____
_____
_____
_____
_____
_____
_____

CREATE AN ILLUSTRATION

Make sure your artwork reflects the situation
in the selection of literature you use for your copywork.

WHAT CAN YOU LEARN ABOUT THE PAST FROM THIS STORY?

8. A CHRISTMAS CAROL

(A Christmas Carol in Prose, Being a Ghost-Story of Christmas)

Genre: Christmas Novella

Author: Charles Dickens

Published: 1843

Charles John Huffam Dickens (February 7, 1812 – June 9, 1870) was an English writer and social critic. He is one of the most popular storytellers of all time. He created some of the world's best-known fictional characters and is regarded as the greatest novelist of the Victorian era. Dickens published more than a dozen major novels, a large number of short stories, including a number of Christmas-themed stories, a handful of plays, and several non-fiction books. Among them are *The Posthumous Papers of the Pickwick Club*, *The Adventures of Oliver Twist*, *A Christmas Carol*, *David Copperfield*, *Little Dorrit*, *A Tale of Two Cities*, and *Our Mutual Friend*.

CHAPTER 3

The moment Scrooge's hand was on the lock, a strange voice called him by his name, and bade him enter. He obeyed.

It was his own room. There was no doubt about that. But it had undergone a surprising transformation. The walls and ceiling were so hung with living green, that it looked a perfect grove; from every part of which, bright gleaming berries glistened. The crisp leaves of holly, mistletoe, and ivy reflected back the light, as if so many little mirrors had been scattered there; and such a mighty blaze went roaring up the chimney, as that dull petrification of a hearth had never known in Scrooge's time, or Marley's, or for many and many a winter season gone. Heaped up on the floor, to form a kind of throne, were turkeys, geese, game, poultry, brawn, great joints of meat, sucking-pigs, long wreaths of sausages, mince-pies, plum-puddings, barrels of oysters, red-hot chestnuts, cherry-cheeked apples, juicy oranges, luscious pears, immense twelfth-cakes, and seething bowls of punch, that made the chamber dim with their delicious steam. In easy state upon this couch, there sat a jolly Giant, glorious to see, who bore a glowing torch, in shape not unlike Plenty's horn, and held it up, high up, to shed its light on Scrooge, as he came peeping round the door.

VOCABULARY QUEST

Highlight and define one interesting or unfamiliar word.

Use a dictionary to explore the meaning of the word.

1._____

_____

CLASSICAL COPYWORK

Copy two paragraphs from any book by this author

Title: _____

Author: _____

Time and Place of Publishing: _____

Names & descriptions of characters:

_____
_____
_____
_____
_____
_____

Copy two paragraphs here:

_____
_____
_____
_____
_____
_____
_____
_____
_____
_____
_____
_____
_____
_____
_____
_____
_____
_____
_____
_____
_____

CREATE AN ILLUSTRATION

Make sure your artwork reflects the situation
in the selection of literature you use for your copywork.

WHAT CAN YOU LEARN ABOUT THE PAST FROM THIS STORY?

9. JANE EYRE

Genre: Gothic Novel
Author: Charlotte Brontë
Published: 1847

Charlotte Brontë (April 21, 1816 – March 31, 1855) was an English novelist and poet. The eldest of the famous three Brontë sisters (Charlotte, Emily, and Anne) who survived into adulthood and whose novels have become classics of English literature. She first published her works under the pen name Currer Bell. Her novels are *Jane Eyre, Shirley, Villette, The Professor,* and *Emma Brown* (unfinished).

CHAPTER 2

The red-room was a square chamber, very seldom slept in, I might say never, indeed, unless when a chance influx of visitors at Gateshead Hall rendered it necessary to turn to account all the accommodation it contained: yet it was one of the largest and stateliest chambers in the mansion. A bed supported on massive pillars of mahogany, hung with curtains of deep red damask, stood out like a tabernacle in the centre; the two large windows, with their blinds always drawn down, were half shrouded in festoons and falls of similar drapery; the carpet was red; the table at the foot of the bed was covered with a crimson cloth; the walls were a soft fawn colour with a blush of pink in it; the wardrobe, the toilet-table, the chairs were of darkly polished old mahogany. Out of these deep surrounding shades rose high, and glared white, the piled-up mattresses and pillows of the bed, spread with a snowy Marseilles counterpane. Scarcely less prominent was an ample cushioned easy-chair near the head of the bed, also white, with a footstool before it; and looking, as I thought, like a pale throne.

This room was chill, because it seldom had a fire; it was silent, because remote from the nursery and kitchen; solemn, because it was known to be so seldom entered. The housemaid alone came here on Saturdays, to wipe from the mirrors and the furniture a week's quiet dust: and Mrs. Reed herself, at far intervals, visited it to review the contents of a certain secret drawer in the wardrobe, where were stored divers parchments, her jewel-casket, and a miniature of her deceased husband; and in those last words lies the secret of the red-room-- the spell which kept it so lonely in spite of its grandeur.

CLASSICAL COPYWORK

Copy two paragraphs from any book by this author

Title: _____

Author: _____

Time and Place of Publishing: _____

Names & descriptions of characters:

_____
_____
_____
_____
_____

Copy two paragraphs here:

_____
_____
_____
_____
_____
_____
_____
_____
_____
_____
_____
_____
_____
_____
_____
_____
_____
_____
_____
_____
_____

CREATE AN ILLUSTRATION

Make sure your artwork reflects the situation
in the selection of literature you use for your copywork.

WHAT CAN YOU LEARN ABOUT THE PAST FROM THIS STORY?

10. WUTHERING HEIGHTS

Genre Tragedy

Author: Emily Brontë

Published: 1847

Emily Jane Brontë (July 30, 1818 – December 19, 1848) was an English novelist and poet who is best known for her only novel, *Wuthering Heights*, now considered a classic of English literature. Emily was the third eldest of the four surviving Brontë siblings, between the youngest Anne, and her brother Branwell. She wrote under the pen name Ellis Bell.

CHAPTER 3

While leading the way upstairs, she recommended that I should hide the candle, and not make a noise; for her master had an odd notion about the chamber she would put me in, and never let anybody lodge there willingly. I asked the reason. She did not know, she answered: she had only lived there a year or two; and they had so many queer goings on, she could not begin to be curious.

Too stupefied to be curious myself, I fastened my door and glanced round for the bed. The whole furniture consisted of a chair, a clothes-press, and a large oak case, with squares cut out near the top resembling coach windows. Having approached this structure, I looked inside, and perceived it to be a singular sort of old-fashioned couch, very conveniently designed to obviate the necessity for every member of the family having a room to himself. In fact, it formed a little closet, and the ledge of a window, which it enclosed, served as a table. I slid back the panelled sides, got in with my light, pulled them together again, and felt secure against the vigilance of Heathcliff, and every one else.

VOCABULARY QUEST

Highlight and define three interesting or unfamiliar words.

Use a dictionary to explore the meaning of each word.

1. _____

_____

2. _____

_____

3. _____

_____

CLASSICAL COPYWORK

Copy two paragraphs from any book by this author

Title: _____

Author: _____

Time and Place of Publishing: _____

Names & descriptions of characters:

_____
_____
_____
_____
_____

Copy two paragraphs here:

_____
_____
_____
_____
_____
_____
_____
_____
_____
_____
_____
_____
_____
_____
_____
_____
_____
_____
_____
_____

CREATE AN ILLUSTRATION

Make sure your artwork reflects the situation
in the selection of literature you use for your copywork.

WHAT CAN YOU LEARN ABOUT THE PAST FROM THIS STORY?

II. THE CHILDREN OF THE NEW FOREST

Genre: Children's Novel

Autho: Frederick Marryat

Published: 1847

Captain Frederick Marryat (July 10, 1792 – August 9, 1848) was a British Royal Navy officer, novelist, and an acquaintance of Charles Dickens. He is known for a widely used system of maritime flag signalling, known as Marryat's Code.

As an author, he is noted as an early pioneer of the sea story. His most notable works are the semi-autobiographical novel *Mr. Midshipman Easy*, his children's novel *The Children of the New Forest*, as well as novels *Poor Jack*, *The Phantom Ship*, and *The Little Savage*.

CHAPTER 3

The next morning, as soon as Jacob had given the children their breakfast, he set off towards Arnwood. He knew that Benjamin had stated his intention to return with the horse and see what had taken place, and he knew him well enough to feel sure that he would do so. He thought it better to see him, if possible, and ascertain the fate of Miss Judith. Jacob arrived at the still smoking ruins of the mansion, and found several people there, mostly residents within a few miles, some attracted by curiosity, others busy in collecting the heavy masses of lead which had been melted from the roof, and appropriating them to their own benefit; but much of it was still too hot to be touched, and they were throwing snow on it to cool it, for it had snowed during the night. At last Jacob perceived Benjamin on horseback riding leisurely towards him, and immediately went up to him.

VOCABULARY QUEST

Highlight and define three interesting or unfamiliar words.

Use a dictionary to explore the meaning of each word.

1. _____

_____

2. _____

_____

3. _____

_____

CLASSICAL COPYWORK

Copy two paragraphs from any book by this author

Title:_____

Author:_____

Time and Place of Publishing:_____

Names & descriptions of characters:

_____
_____
_____
_____
_____

Copy two paragraphs here:

_____
_____
_____
_____
_____
_____
_____
_____
_____
_____
_____
_____
_____
_____
_____
_____
_____
_____
_____

CREATE AN ILLUSTRATION

Make sure your artwork reflects the situation
in the selection of literature you use for your copywork.

WHAT CAN YOU LEARN ABOUT THE PAST FROM THIS STORY?

12. DAVID COPPERFIELD

(Full title: *The Personal History, Adventures, Experience and Observation of David Copperfield the Younger of Blunderstone Rookery (which he never meant to publish on any account)*)

Genre: Novel (Bildungsroman)

Author: Charles Dickens

Published: 1849-1850 (as a serial) and 1850 (as a book)

Charles John Huffam Dickens (February 7, 1812 – June 9, 1870) was an English writer and social critic. He is one of the most popular storytellers of all time. He created some of the world's best-known fictional characters and is regarded as the greatest novelist of the Victorian era. Dickens published more than a dozen major novels, a large number of short stories, including a number of Christmas-themed stories, a handful of plays, and several non-fiction books. Among them are *The Posthumous Papers of the Pickwick Club, The Adventures of Oliver Twist, A Christmas Carol, David Copperfield, Little Dorrit, A Tale of Two Cities,* and *Our Mutual Friend.*

CHAPTER 64

And now my written story ends. I look back, once more—for the last time—before I close these leaves. I see myself, with Agnes at my side, journeying along the road of life. I see our children and our friends around us; and I hear the roar of many voices, not indifferent to me as I travel on.

What faces are the most distinct to me in the fleeting crowd? Lo, these; all turning to me as I ask my thoughts the question! Here is my aunt, in stronger spectacles, an old woman of four-score years and more, but upright yet, and a steady walker of six miles at a stretch in winter weather.

Always with her, here comes Peggotty, my good old nurse, likewise in spectacles, accustomed to do needle-work at night very close to the lamp, but never sitting down to it without a bit of wax candle, a yard-measure in a little house, and a work-box with a picture of St. Paul's upon the lid.

VOCABULARY QUEST

Highlight and define one interesting or unfamiliar word.

Use a dictionary to explore the meaning of the word.

1._____

_____

CLASSICAL COPYWORK

Copy two paragraphs from any book by this author

Title: _____

Author: _____

Time and Place of Publishing: _____

Names & descriptions of characters:

_____
_____
_____
_____
_____

Copy two paragraphs here:

_____
_____
_____
_____
_____
_____
_____
_____
_____
_____
_____
_____
_____
_____
_____
_____
_____
_____
_____
_____

CREATE AN ILLUSTRATION

Make sure your artwork reflects the situation
in the selection of literature you use for your copywork.

WHAT CAN YOU LEARN ABOUT THE PAST FROM THIS STORY?

13. ALICE IN WONDERLAND

(Alice's Adventures in Wonderland)

Genre: Novel (Children's Fiction)

Author: Lewis Carroll

Published: 1865

Charles Lutwidge Dodgson (January 27, 1832 – January 14, 1898), better known by his pen name Lewis Carroll, was an English writer, mathematician,

logician, Anglican deacon, and photographer. His most famous works are *Alice's Adventures in Wonderland*, its sequel *Through the Looking-Glass*, *A Tangled Tale*, *Sylvie and Bruno*, the poems *Jabberwocky*, and the *The Hunting of the Snark*, all examples of the genre of literary nonsense. He is noted for his facility at word play, logic, and fantasy.

CHAPTER 1 – DOWN THE RABBIT-HOLE

Suddenly she came upon a little three-legged table, all made of solid glass; there was nothing on it except a tiny golden key, and Alice's first thought was that it might belong to one of the doors of the hall; but, alas! either the locks were too large, or the key was too small, but at any rate it would not open any of them. However, on the second time round, she came upon a low curtain she had not noticed before, and behind it was a little door about fifteen inches high: she tried the little golden key in the lock, and to her great delight it fitted!

Alice opened the door and found that it led into a small passage, not much larger than a rat-hole: she knelt down and looked along the passage into the loveliest garden you ever saw. How she longed to get out of that dark hall, and wander about among those beds of bright flowers and those cool fountains, but she could not even get her head through the doorway; `and even if my head would go through,' thought poor Alice, `it would be of very little use without my shoulders. Oh, how I wish I could shut up like a telescope! I think I could, if I only know how to begin.' For, you see, so many out-of-the-way things had happened lately, that Alice had begun to think that very few things indeed were really impossible.

VOCABULARY QUEST

Highlight and define one interesting or unfamiliar word.

Use a dictionary to explore the meaning of the word.

1._____

_____

CLASSICAL COPYWORK

Copy two paragraphs from any book by this author

Title: _____

Author: _____

Time and Place of Publishing: _____

Names & descriptions of characters:

_____
_____
_____
_____
_____

Copy two paragraphs here:

_____
_____
_____
_____
_____
_____
_____
_____
_____
_____
_____
_____
_____
_____
_____
_____
_____
_____

CREATE AN ILLUSTRATION

Make sure your artwork reflects the situation
in the selection of literature you use for your copywork.

WHAT CAN YOU LEARN ABOUT THE PAST FROM THIS STORY?

14. THROUGH THE LOOKING-GLASS

(Through the Looking-Glass and What Alice Found There)

Genre: Novel (Children's Fiction)

Author: Lewis Carroll

Published: 1871

Charles Lutwidge Dodgson (January 27, 1832 – January 14, 1898), better known by his pen name Lewis Carroll, was an English writer, mathematician, logician, Anglican deacon, and photographer. His most famous works are *Alice's Adventures in Wonderland*, its sequel *Through the Looking-Glass*, *A Tangled Tale*, *Sylvie and Bruno*, the poems *Jabberwocky*, and the *The Hunting of the Snark*, all examples of the genre of literary nonsense. He is noted for his facility at word play, logic, and fantasy.

CHAPTER 7 – THE LION AND THE UNICORN

The next moment soldiers came running through the wood, at first in twos and threes, then ten or twenty together, and at last in such crowds that they seemed to fill the whole forest. Alice got behind a tree, for fear of being run over, and watched them go by.

She thought that in all her life she had never seen soldiers so uncertain on their feet: they were always tripping over something or other, and whenever one went down, several more always fell over him, so that the ground was soon covered with little heaps of men.

Then came the horses. Having four feet, these managed rather better than the foot-soldiers: but even they stumbled now and then; and it seemed to be a regular rule that, whenever a horse stumbled the rider fell off instantly. The confusion got worse every moment, and Alice was very glad to get out of the wood into an open place, where she found the White King seated on the ground, busily writing in his memorandum-book.

VOCABULARY QUEST

Highlight and define two interesting or unfamiliar words.

Use a dictionary to explore the meaning of each word.

1. _____

   _____

2. _____

   _____

CLASSICAL COPYWORK

Copy two paragraphs from any book by this author

Title: _____

Author: _____

Time and Place of Publishing: _____

Names & descriptions of characters:

_____
_____
_____
_____
_____
_____

Copy two paragraphs here:

_____
_____
_____
_____
_____
_____
_____
_____
_____
_____
_____
_____
_____
_____
_____
_____
_____
_____
_____
_____

CREATE AN ILLUSTRATION

Make sure your artwork reflects the situation
in the selection of literature you use for your copywork.

WHAT CAN YOU LEARN ABOUT THE PAST FROM THIS STORY?

15. TREASURE ISLAND

Genre: Adventure Novel

Author: Robert Louis Stevenson

Published: 1883 (as a book)

Robert Louis Stevenson (November 13, 1850 – December 3, 1894) was a Scottish novelist, poet, essayist, and travel writer.

A literary celebrity during his lifetime, he now ranks among the 26 most translated authors in the world. His most famous works are *Treasure Island*, *Kidnapped*, *Strange Case of Dr Jekyll and Mr Hyde*, *The Black Arrow: A Tale of the Two Roses*, and *New Arabian Nights*.

CHAPTER 14 – THE FIRST BLOW

I now felt for the first time the joy of exploration. The isle was uninhabited; my shipmates I had left behind, and nothing lived in front of me but dumb brutes and fowls. I turned hither and thither among the trees. Here and there were flowering plants, unknown to me; here and there I saw snakes, and one raised his head from a ledge of rock and hissed at me with a noise not unlike the spinning of a top. Little did I suppose that he was a deadly enemy and that the noise was the famous rattle.

Then I came to a long thicket of these oak-*like* trees – live, or evergreen, oaks, I heard afterwards they should be called – *which grew low along the sand like brambles*, the boughs curiously twisted, the foliage compact, *like* thatch. The thicket stretched down from the top of one of the sandy knolls, spreading and growing taller as it went, until it reached the margin of the broad, reedy fen, through which the nearest of the little rivers soaked its way into the anchorage. The marsh was steaming in the strong sun, and the outline of the Spy-glass trembled through the haze.

VOCABULARY QUEST

Highlight and define three interesting or unfamiliar words.

Use a dictionary to explore the meaning of each word.

1. _____

_____

2. _____

_____

3. _____

_____

CLASSICAL COPYWORK

Copy two paragraphs from any book by this author

Title: _____

Author: _____

Time and Place of Publishing: _____

Names & descriptions of characters:

_____
_____
_____
_____
_____

Copy two paragraphs here:

_____
_____
_____
_____
_____
_____
_____
_____
_____
_____
_____
_____
_____
_____
_____
_____
_____
_____

CREATE AN ILLUSTRATION

Make sure your artwork reflects the situation
in the selection of literature you use for your copywork.

WHAT CAN YOU LEARN ABOUT THE PAST FROM THIS STORY?

16. STRANGE CASE OF DR JEKYLL AND MR HYDE

Genre: Novella (Horror, Gothic, and Science Fiction)

Author: Robert Louis Stevenson

Published: 1886

Robert Louis Stevenson (November 13, 1850 – December 3, 1894) was a Scottish novelist, poet, essayist, and travel writer.

A literary celebrity during his lifetime, he now ranks among the 26 most translated authors in the world. His most famous works are *Treasure Island, Kidnapped, Strange Case of Dr Jekyll and Mr Hyde, The Black Arrow: A Tale of the Two Roses,* and *New Arabian Nights.*

CHAPTER 6 – INCIDENT OF DR. LANYON

Time ran on; thousands of pounds were offered in reward, for the death of Sir Danvers was resented as a public injury; but Mr. Hyde had disappeared out of the ken of the police as though he had never existed. Much of his past was unearthed, indeed, and all disreputable: tales came out of the man's cruelty, at once so callous and violent; of his vile life, of his strange associates, of the hatred that seemed to have surrounded his career; but of his present whereabouts, not a whisper. From the time he had left the house in Soho on the morning of the murder, he was simply blotted out; and gradually, as time drew on, Mr. Utterson began to recover from the hotness of his alarm, and to grow more at quiet with himself. The death of Sir Danvers was, to his way of thinking, more than paid for by the disappearance of Mr. Hyde. Now that that evil influence had been withdrawn, a new life began for Dr. Jekyll. He came out of his seclusion, renewed relations with his friends, became once more their familiar guest and entertainer; and whilst he had always been known for charities, he was now no less distinguished for religion. He was busy, he was much in the open air, he did good; his face seemed to open and brighten, as if with an inward consciousness of service; and for more than two months, the doctor was at peace.

VOCABULARY QUEST

Highlight and define two interesting or unfamiliar words.

Use a dictionary to explore the meaning of each word.

1. _____

_____

2. _____

_____

CLASSICAL COPYWORK

Copy two paragraphs from any book by this author

Title: _____

Author: _____

Time and Place of Publishing: _____

Names & descriptions of characters:

_____
_____
_____
_____
_____

Copy two paragraphs here:

_____
_____
_____
_____
_____
_____
_____
_____
_____
_____
_____
_____
_____
_____
_____
_____
_____
_____
_____
_____

CREATE AN ILLUSTRATION

Make sure your artwork reflects the situation
in the selection of literature you use for your copywork.

WHAT CAN YOU LEARN ABOUT THE PAST FROM THIS STORY?

17. THREE MEN IN A BOAT

(To Say Nothing of the Dog)

Genre: Comedy Novel

Author: Jerome K. Jerome

Published: 1889

Jerome Klapka Jerome (May 2, 1859 – June 14, 1927) was an English writer and humorist, best known for the comic travelogue *Three Men in a Boat*.

His other famous works include the essay collections *Idle Thoughts of an Idle Fellow* and *Second Thoughts of an Idle Fellow*, *Three Men on the Bummel*, *Packing for the Journey*, *All Roads Lead to Calvary*, *Paul Kelver*, and several other novels.

CHAPTER 10

How good one feels when one is full—how satisfied with ourselves and with the world! People who have tried it, tell me that a clear conscience makes you very happy and contented; but a full stomach does the business quite as well, and is cheaper, and more easily obtained. One feels so forgiving and generous after a substantial and well-digested meal—so noble-minded, so kindly-hearted.

It is very strange, this domination of our intellect by our digestive organs. We cannot work, we cannot think, unless our stomach wills so. It dictates to us our emotions, our passions. After eggs and bacon, it says, "Work!" After beefsteak and porter, it says, "Sleep!" After a cup of tea (two spoonsful for each cup, and don't let it stand more than three minutes), it says to the brain, "Now, rise, and show your strength. Be eloquent, and deep, and tender; see, with a clear eye, into Nature and into life; spread your white wings of quivering thought, and soar, a god-like spirit, over the whirling world beneath you, up through long lanes of flaming stars to the gates of eternity!"

VOCABULARY QUEST

Highlight and define three interesting or unfamiliar words.

Use a dictionary to explore the meaning of each word.

1._____

_____

2._____

_____

3._____

_____

CLASSICAL COPYWORK

Copy two paragraphs from any book by this author

Title: _____

Author: _____

Time and Place of Publishing: _____

Names & descriptions of characters:

_____
_____
_____
_____
_____
_____

Copy two paragraphs here:

_____
_____
_____
_____
_____
_____
_____
_____
_____
_____
_____
_____
_____
_____
_____
_____
_____
_____
_____
_____
_____

CREATE AN ILLUSTRATION

Make sure your artwork reflects the situation
in the selection of literature you use for your copywork.

WHAT CAN YOU LEARN ABOUT THE PAST FROM THIS STORY?

18. THE SIGN OF THE FOUR

Genre: Novel (Detective Fiction)

Author: Sir Arthur Conan Doyle

Published: 1890

Sir Arthur Ignatius Conan Doyle (May 22, 1859 – July 7, 1930) was a British physician and prolific writer whose works include fantasy and science fiction, detectives stories, plays, romances, poetry, non-fiction, and historical novels.

Conan Doyle is most noted for creating the fictional detective Sherlock Holmes and writing stories about him which are generally considered milestones in the field of crime fiction.

He is also known for writing the fictional adventures of a second character he invented, Professor Challenger. The author's most notable works are *Stories of Sherlock Holmes* and *The Lost World*.

CHAPTER 2 – THE STATEMENT OF THE CASE

"I have not yet described to you the most singular part. About six years ago -- to be exact, upon the fourth of May, 1882 -- an advertisement appeared in the Times asking for the address of Miss Mary Morstan, and stating that it would be to her advantage to come forward. There was no name or address appended. I had at that time just entered the family of Mrs. Cecil Forrester in the capacity of governess. By her advice I published my address in the advertisement column. The same day there arrived through the post a small cardboard box addressed to me, which I found to contain a very large and lustrous pearl. No word of writing was enclosed. Since then every year upon the same date there has always appeared a similar box, containing a similar pearl, without any clue as to the sender. They have been pronounced by an expert to be of a rare variety and of considerable value. You can see for yourself that they are very handsome."

She opened a flat box as she spoke and showed me six of the finest pearls that I had ever seen.

VOCABULARY QUEST

Highlight and define three interesting or unfamiliar words.

Use a dictionary to explore the meaning of each word.

1._____

_____

2._____

_____

CLASSICAL COPYWORK

Copy two paragraphs from any book by this author

Title: _____

Author: _____

Time and Place of Publishing: _____

Names & descriptions of characters:

_____
_____
_____
_____
_____
_____

Copy two paragraphs here:

_____
_____
_____
_____
_____
_____
_____
_____
_____
_____
_____
_____
_____
_____
_____
_____
_____
_____
_____
_____

CREATE AN ILLUSTRATION

Make sure your artwork reflects the situation
in the selection of literature you use for your copywork.

WHAT CAN YOU LEARN ABOUT THE PAST FROM THIS STORY?

19. THE PICTURE OF DORIAN GRAY

Genre: Philosophical Novel

Author: Oscar Wilde

Published: 1890

Oscar Fingal O'Flahertie Wills Wilde (October 16, 1854 – November 30, 1900) was an Irish playwright novelist, essayist, poet, and a spokesman for aestheticism. After writing in different forms throughout the 1880s, he became one of London's most popular playwrights in the early 1890s. He is remembered for his epigrams, his novel *The Picture of Dorian Gray*, his plays, especially *The Importance of Being Earnest* and *A Woman of No Importance*, and his fairy stories *Lord Arthur Savile's Crime and Other Stories*, *House of Pomegranates*, and *The Happy Prince and Other Stories*.

CHAPTER 1

Then he looked at Lord Henry. "Dorian Gray is my dearest friend," he said. "He has a simple and a beautiful nature. Your aunt was quite right in what she said of him. Don't spoil him. Don't try to influence him. Your influence would be bad. The world is wide, and has many marvelous people in it. Don't take away from me the one person who gives to my art whatever charm it possesses: my life as an artist depends on him. Mind, Harry, I trust you." He spoke very slowly, and the words seemed wrung out of him almost against his will.

VOCABULARY QUEST

Highlight and define five interesting or unfamiliar words.

Use a dictionary to explore the meaning of each word.

1. _____

_____

2. _____

_____

3. _____

_____

4. _____

_____

5. _____

_____

CLASSICAL COPYWORK

Copy two paragraphs from any book by this author

Title: _____

Author: _____

Time and Place of Publishing: _____

Names & descriptions of characters:

_____
_____
_____
_____
_____
_____

Copy two paragraphs here:

_____
_____
_____
_____
_____
_____
_____
_____
_____
_____
_____
_____
_____
_____
_____
_____
_____
_____
_____
_____
_____
_____

CREATE AN ILLUSTRATION

Make sure your artwork reflects the situation
in the selection of literature you use for your copywork.

WHAT CAN YOU LEARN ABOUT THE PAST FROM THIS STORY?

20. THE JUNGLE BOOK

Genre: Children's Book

Author: Rudyard Kipling

Published: 1894

Joseph Rudyard Kipling (December 30, 1865 – January 18, 1936) was an English journalist, short-story writer, poet, and novelist. He is regarded as a major innovator in the art of the short story. His children's books are classics of children's literature. In the late 19th and early 20th centuries, Kipling was one of the most popular writers in the United Kingdom, in both prose and verse, In 1907. he was awarded the Nobel Prize in Literature, making him the first English-language writer to receive the prize.

Kipling's most notable works include *The Jungle Book*, *Kim*, *Just So Stories*, and *Captains Courageous*. His poems include "Mandalay," "The Gods of the Copybook Headings," and "If."

CHAPTER 1 - MOWGLI'S BROTHERS

It was seven o'clock of a very warm evening in the Seeonee hills when Father Wolf woke up from his day's rest, scratched himself, yawned, and spread out his paws one after the other to get rid of the sleepy feeling in their tips. Mother Wolf lay with her big gray nose dropped across her four tumbling, squealing cubs, and the moon shone into the mouth of the cave where they all lived. "Augrh!" said Father Wolf. "It is time to hunt again." He was going to spring down hill when a little shadow with a bushy tail crossed the threshold and whined: "Good luck go with you, O Chief of the Wolves. And good luck and strong white teeth go with noble children that they may never forget the hungry in this world."

It was the jackal—Tabaqui, the Dish-licker—and the wolves of India despise Tabaqui because he runs about making mischief, and telling tales, and eating rags and pieces of leather from the village rubbish-heaps. But they are afraid of him too, because Tabaqui, more than anyone else in the jungle, is apt to go mad, and then he forgets that he was ever afraid of anyone, and runs through the forest biting everything in his way. Even the tiger runs and hides when little Tabaqui goes mad, for madness is the most disgraceful thing that can overtake a wild creature. We call it hydrophobia, but they call it dewanee—the madness—and run.

VOCABULARY QUEST

Highlight and define one interesting or unfamiliar word.

Use a dictionary to explore the meaning of the word.

1. _____

_____

CLASSICAL COPYWORK

Copy two paragraphs from any book by this author

Title: _____

Author: _____

Time and Place of Publishing: _____

Names & descriptions of characters:

_____
_____
_____
_____
_____

Copy two paragraphs here:

_____
_____
_____
_____
_____
_____
_____
_____
_____
_____
_____
_____
_____
_____
_____
_____
_____
_____
_____

CREATE AN ILLUSTRATION

Make sure your artwork reflects the situation
in the selection of literature you use for your copywork.

WHAT CAN YOU LEARN ABOUT THE PAST FROM THIS STORY?

21. THE PRISONER OF ZENDA

Genre: Adventure Novel

Author: Anthony Hope

Published: 1894

Sir Anthony Hope Hawkins, better known as Anthony Hope (February 9, 1863 – July 8, 1933), was an English novelist and playwright. He was a prolific writer, especially of adventure novels, but he is remembered best for only two books: *The Prisoner of Zenda* (1894) and its sequel *Rupert of Hentzau* (1898). These works, "minor classics" of English literature, are set in the contemporaneous fictional country of Ruritania and spawned the genre known as Ruritanian romance.

CHAPTER 3 - A MERRY MEETING WITH A DISTANT RELATIVE

I opened my eyes, and found two men regarding me with much curiosity. Both wore shooting costumes and carried guns. One was rather short and very stoutly built, with a big bullet-shaped head, a bristly grey moustache, and small pale-blue eyes, a trifle blood-shot. The other was a slender young fellow, of middle height, dark in complexion, and bearing himself with grace and distinction. I set the one down as an old soldier: the other for a gentleman accustomed to move in good society, but not unused to military life either. It turned out afterwards that my guess was a good one.

The elder man approached me, beckoning the younger to follow. He did so, courteously raising his hat. I rose slowly to my feet.

VOCABULARY QUEST

Highlight and define three interesting or unfamiliar words.

Use a dictionary to explore the meaning of each word.

1. _____

_____

2. _____

_____

3. _____

_____

CLASSICAL COPYWORK

Copy two paragraphs from any book by this author

Title: _____

Author: _____

Time and Place of Publishing: _____

Names & descriptions of characters:

_____
_____
_____
_____
_____

Copy two paragraphs here:

_____
_____
_____
_____
_____
_____
_____
_____
_____
_____
_____
_____
_____
_____
_____
_____
_____
_____
_____

CREATE AN ILLUSTRATION

Make sure your artwork reflects the situation
in the selection of literature you use for your copywork.

WHAT CAN YOU LEARN ABOUT THE PAST FROM THIS STORY?

22. THE TIME MACHINE

Genre: Science Fiction Novel

Author: H. G. Wells

Published: 1895

Herbert George Wells (September 21, 1866 – August 13, 1946) was a prolific English writer in many genres, including the novel, history, politics, social commentary, textbooks and rules for war games. Wells is now best remembered for his science fiction novels and is called the father of science fiction. His most notable science fiction works include *The Time Machine* (1895), *The Island of Doctor Moreau* (1896), *The Invisible Man* (1897), and *The War of the Worlds* (1898).

Wells is generally credited with the popularization of the concept of time travel by using a vehicle that allows an operator to travel purposely and selectively forward or backward in time.

He was nominated for the Nobel Prize in Literature four times.

CHAPTER 2

I think that at that time none of us quite believed in the Time Machine. The fact is, the Time Traveller was one of those men who are too clever to be believed: you never felt that you saw all round him; you always suspected some subtle reserve, some ingenuity in ambush, behind his lucid frankness. Had Filby shown the model and explained the matter in the Time Traveller's words, we should have shown HIM far less scepticism. For we should have perceived his motives; a pork butcher could understand Filby. But the Time Traveller had more than a touch of whim among his elements, and we distrusted him. Things that would have made the frame of a less clever man seemed tricks in his hands. It is a mistake to do things too easily. The serious people who took him seriously never felt quite sure of his deportment; they were somehow aware that trusting their reputations for judgment with him was like furnishing a nursery with egg-shell china. So I don't think any of us said very much about time travelling in the interval between that Thursday and the next, though its odd potentialities ran, no doubt, in most of our minds: its plausibility, that is, its practical incredibleness, the curious possibilities of anachronism and of utter confusion it suggested. For my own part, I was particularly preoccupied with the trick of the model. That I remember discussing with the Medical Man, whom I met on Friday at the Linnaean. He said he had seen a similar thing at Tubingen, and laid considerable stress on the blowing out of the candle. But how the trick was done he could not explain.

CLASSICAL COPYWORK

Copy two paragraphs from any book by this author

Title: _____

Author: _____

Time and Place of Publishing: _____

Names & descriptions of characters:

_____
_____
_____
_____
_____

Copy two paragraphs here:

_____
_____
_____
_____
_____
_____
_____
_____
_____
_____
_____
_____
_____
_____
_____
_____
_____
_____
_____

CREATE AN ILLUSTRATION

Make sure your artwork reflects the situation
in the selection of literature you use for your copywork.

WHAT CAN YOU LEARN ABOUT THE PAST FROM THIS STORY?

23. THE WAR OF THE WORLDS

Genre: Science Fiction Novel

Author: H. G. Wells

Published: 1898

Herbert George Wells (September 21, 1866 – August 13, 1946) was a prolific English writer in many genres, including the novel, history, politics, social commentary, textbooks and rules for war games. Wells is now best remembered for his science fiction novels and is called the father of science fiction. His most notable science fiction works include *The Time Machine* (1895), *The Island of Doctor Moreau* (1896), *The Invisible Man* (1897), and *The War of the Worlds* (1898).

Wells is generally credited with the popularization of the concept of time travel by using a vehicle that allows an operator to travel purposely and selectively forward or backward in time.

He was nominated for the Nobel Prize in Literature four times.

BOOK 1
CHAPTER 1 - THE EVE OF THE WAR

No one would have believed in the last years of the nineteenth century that this world was being watched keenly and closely by intelligences greater than man's and yet as mortal as his own; that as men busied themselves about their various concerns they were scrutinised and studied, perhaps almost as narrowly as a man with a microscope might scrutinise the transient creatures that swarm and multiply in a drop of water. With infinite complacency men went to and fro over this globe about their little affairs, serene in their assurance of their empire over matter. It is possible that the infusoria under the microscope do the same. No one gave a thought to the older worlds of space as sources of human danger, or thought of them only to dismiss the idea of life upon them as impossible or improbable. It is curious to recall some of the mental habits of those departed days. At most terrestrial men fancied there might be other men upon Mars, perhaps inferior to themselves and ready to welcome a missionary enterprise. Yet across the gulf of space, minds that are to our minds as ours are to those of the beasts that perish, intellects vast and cool and unsympathetic, regarded this earth with envious eyes, and slowly and surely drew their plans against us. And early in the twentieth century came the great disillusionment.

CLASSICAL COPYWORK

Copy two paragraphs from any book by this author

Title: _____

Author: _____

Time and Place of Publishing: _____

Names & descriptions of characters:

_____
_____
_____
_____
_____

Copy two paragraphs here:

_____
_____
_____
_____
_____
_____
_____
_____
_____
_____
_____
_____
_____
_____
_____
_____
_____
_____
_____

CREATE AN ILLUSTRATION

Make sure your artwork reflects the situation
in the selection of literature you use for your copywork.

WHAT CAN YOU LEARN ABOUT THE PAST FROM THIS STORY?

24. MOONFLEET

Genre: Adventure Novel

Author: J. Meade Falkner

Published: 1898

John Meade Falkner (May 8, 1858 – July 22, 1932) was an English novelist and poet, best known for his 1898 novel, *Moonfleet*. As well as being an extremely successful businessman, he became chairman of the arms manufacturer Armstrong Whitworth during World War I. His novels are *The Lost Stradivarius* (1895), *Moonfleet* (1898), and *The Nebuly Coat* (1903). In addition to his three novels and his poetry, he also wrote three topographical guides (Oxfordshire, Bath, and Berkshire) and a *History of Oxfordshire*.

CHAPTER 1 - IN MOONFLEET VILLAGE

At last the light began to fail, and I was nothing loth to leave off reading for several reasons; as, first, the parlour was a chilly room with horse-hair chairs and sofa, and only a coloured-paper screen in the grate, for my aunt did not allow a fire till the first of November; second, there was a rank smell of molten tallow in the house, for my aunt was dipping winter candles on frames in the back kitchen; third, I had reached a part in the Arabian Nights which tightened my breath and made me wish to leave off reading for very anxiousness of expectation. It was that point in the story of the 'Wonderful Lamp', where the false uncle lets fall a stone that seals the mouth of the underground chamber; and immures the boy, Aladdin, in the darkness, because he would not give up the lamp till he stood safe on the surface again. This scene reminded me of one of those dreadful nightmares, where we dream we are shut in a little room, the walls of which are closing in upon us, and so impressed me that the memory of it served as a warning in an adventure that befell me later on. So I gave up reading and stepped out into the street. It was a poor street at best, though once, no doubt, it had been finer. Now, there were not two hundred souls in Moonfleet, and yet the houses that held them straggled sadly over half a mile, lying at intervals along either side of the road. Nothing was ever made new in the village; if a house wanted repair badly, it was pulled down, and so there were toothless gaps in the street, and overrun gardens with broken-down walls, and many of the houses that yet stood looked as though they could stand but little longer.

CLASSICAL COPYWORK

Copy two paragraphs from any book by this author

Title: _____

Author: _____

Time and Place of Publishing: _____

Names & descriptions of characters:

_____
_____
_____
_____
_____
_____

Copy two paragraphs here:

_____
_____
_____
_____
_____
_____
_____
_____
_____
_____
_____
_____
_____
_____
_____
_____
_____
_____
_____

CREATE AN ILLUSTRATION

Make sure your artwork reflects the situation
in the selection of literature you use for your copywork.

WHAT CAN YOU LEARN ABOUT THE PAST FROM THIS STORY?

25. KIM

Genre: Spy & Picaresque Novel

Author: Rudyard Kipling

Published: 1901

Joseph Rudyard Kipling (December 30, 1865 – January 18, 1936) was an English journalist, short-story writer, poet, and novelist. He is regarded as a major innovator in the art of the short story. His children's books are now considered classics of children's literature. In the late 19th and 20th centuries, Kipling was one of the most popular writers in the United Kingdom, in both prose and verse. In 1907, he was awarded the Nobel Prize in Literature, making him the first English-language writer to receive the prize.

Kipling's most notable works include *The Jungle Book*, *Kim*, *Just So Stories*, and *Captains Courageous*. His poems include "Mandalay," "The Gods of the Copybook Headings," and "If."

CHAPTER 4

The diamond-bright dawn woke men and crows and bullocks together. Kim sat up and yawned, shook himself, and thrilled with delight. This was seeing the world in real truth; this was life as he would have it bustling and shouting, the buckling of belts, and beating of bullocks and creaking of wheels, lighting of fires and cooking of food, and new sights at every turn of the approving eye. The morning mist swept off in a whorl of silver, the parrots shot away to some distant river in shrieking green hosts: all the well-wheels within ear-shot went to work. India was awake, and Kim was in the middle of it, more awake and more excited than anyone, chewing on a twig that he would presently use as a toothbrush; for he borrowed right- and left-handedly from all the customs of the country he knew and loved. There was no need to worry about food no need to spend a cowrie at the crowded stalls. He was the disciple of a holy man annexed by a strong-willed old lady. All things would be prepared for them, and when they were respectfully invited so to do they would sit and eat.

VOCABULARY QUEST

Highlight and define two interesting or unfamiliar words.

Use a dictionary to explore the meaning of each word.

1. _____

_____

2. _____

_____

CLASSICAL COPYWORK

Copy two paragraphs from any book by this author

Title: _____

Author: _____

Time and Place of Publishing: _____

Names & descriptions of characters:

_____
_____
_____
_____
_____
_____

Copy two paragraphs here:

_____
_____
_____
_____
_____
_____
_____
_____
_____
_____
_____
_____
_____
_____
_____
_____
_____
_____
_____
_____
_____
_____

CREATE AN ILLUSTRATION

Make sure your artwork reflects the situation
in the selection of literature you use for your copywork.

WHAT CAN YOU LEARN ABOUT THE PAST FROM THIS STORY?

26. THE HOUND OF THE BASKERVILLES

Genre: Detective Fiction (Crime Novel)

Author: Sir Arthur Conan Doyle

Published: 1902

Sir Arthur Ignatius Conan Doyle (May 22, 1859 – July 7, 1930) was a British physician and prolific writer whose works include fantasy and science fiction, detectives stories, plays, romances, poetry, non-fiction, and historical novels.

Conan Doyle is most noted for creating the fictional detective Sherlock Holmes and writing stories about him which are generally considered milestones in the field of crime fiction.

He is also known for writing the fictional adventures of a second character that he invented, Professor Challenger. The author's most notable works are *Stories of Sherlock Holmes* and *The Lost World*.

CHAPTER 14 – THE HOUND OF THE BASKERVILLES

One of Sherlock Holmes's defects -- if, indeed, one may call it a defect -- was that he was exceedingly loath to communicate his full plans to any other person until the instant of their fulfilment. Partly it came no doubt from his own masterful nature, which loved to dominate and surprise those who were around him. Partly also from his professional caution, which urged him never to take any chances. The result, however, was very trying for those who were acting as his agents and assistants. I had often suffered under it, but never more so than during that long drive in the darkness. The great ordeal was in front of us; at last we were about to make our final effort, and yet Holmes had said nothing, and I could only surmise what his course of action would be. My nerves thrilled with anticipation when at last the cold wind upon our faces and the dark, void spaces on either side of the narrow road told me that we were back upon the moor once again. Every stride of the horses and every turn of the wheels was taking us nearer to our supreme adventure

VOCABULARY QUEST

Highlight and define two interesting or unfamiliar words.

Use a dictionary to explore the meaning of each word.

1. _____

_____

2. _____

_____

CLASSICAL COPYWORK

Copy two paragraphs from any book by this author

Title: _____

Author: _____

Time and Place of Publishing: _____

Names & descriptions of characters:

_____
_____
_____
_____
_____
_____

Copy two paragraphs here:

_____
_____
_____
_____
_____
_____
_____
_____
_____
_____
_____
_____
_____
_____
_____
_____
_____
_____
_____
_____

CREATE AN ILLUSTRATION

Make sure your artwork reflects the situation
in the selection of literature you use for your copywork.

WHAT CAN YOU LEARN ABOUT THE PAST FROM THIS STORY?

27. THE SCARLET PIMPERNEL

Genre: Adventure Novel

Author: Emma Orczy

Published: 1905

Baroness Emma "Emmuska" Orczy de Orci (September 23, 1865 – November 12, 1947) was a Hungarian-born British novelist, playwright, and artist of noble origin. She is most known for her series of novels featuring the Scarlet Pimpernel. Her most notable works are *The Scarlet Pimpernel (play 1903, novel 1905)*, *I Will Repay*, *Eldorado*, *The Triumph of the Scarlet Pimpernel*, *The Way of the Scarlet Pimpernel*, *Sir Percy Leads the Band*, and *Mam'zelle Guillotine*.

CHAPTER 2 - DOVER: "THE FISHERMAN'S REST"

The coffee-room of "The Fisherman's Rest" is a show place now at the beginning of the twentieth century. At the end of the eighteenth, in the year of grace 1792, it had not yet gained the notoriety and importance which a hundred additional years and the craze of the age have since bestowed upon it. Yet it was an old place, even then, for the oak rafters and beams were already black with age--as were the panelled seats, with their tall backs, and the long polished tables between, on which innumerable pewter tankards had left fantastic patterns of many-sized rings. In the leaded window, high up, a row of pots of scarlet geraniums and blue larkspur gave the bright note of colour against the dull background of the oak

---

VOCABULARY QUEST

Highlight and define five interesting or unfamiliar words.

Use a dictionary to explore the meaning of each word.

1. _____

_____

2. _____

_____

3. _____

_____

4. _____

_____

5. _____

_____

CLASSICAL COPYWORK

Copy two paragraphs from any book by this author

Title: _____

Author: _____

Time and Place of Publishing: _____

Names & descriptions of characters:

_____
_____
_____
_____
_____
_____

Copy two paragraphs here:

_____
_____
_____
_____
_____
_____
_____
_____
_____
_____
_____
_____
_____
_____
_____
_____
_____
_____
_____

CREATE AN ILLUSTRATION

Make sure your artwork reflects the situation
in the selection of literature you use for your copywork.

WHAT CAN YOU LEARN ABOUT THE PAST FROM THIS STORY?

28. PETER PAN

(or The Boy Who Wouldn't Grow Up or Peter and Wendy)

Genre: Novel

Author: J. M. Barrie

Published: 1911

Sir James Matthew Barrie, 1st Baronet (May 9, 1860 – June 19, 1937) was a Scottish novelist and playwright, best remembered today as the creator of Peter Pan. He wrote a number of successful novels and plays including *The Little White Bird* and *Peter Pan, or The Boy Who Wouldn't Grow Up,* which was originally a stage play, then later released as the novel *Peter Pan.* Although he continued to write successfully, *Peter Pan* overshadowed his other works. He is also credited with popularizing the then-uncommon name Wendy.

Barrie was made a baronet by George V in June 14, 1913 and a member of the Order of Merit in the 1922 New Year Honours.

CHAPTER 1: PETER BREAKS THROUGH

All children, except one, grow up. They soon know that they will grow up, and the way Wendy knew was this. One day when she was two years old she was playing in a garden, and she plucked another flower and ran with it to her mother. I suppose she must have looked rather delightful, for Mrs. Darling put her hand to her heart and cried, "Oh, why can't you remain like this for ever!" This was all that passed between them on the subject, but henceforth Wendy knew that she must grow up. You always know after you are two. Two is the beginning of the end.

Of course they lived at 14 [their house number on their street], and until Wendy came her mother was the chief one. She was a lovely lady, with a romantic mind and such a sweet mocking mouth. Her romantic mind was like the tiny boxes, one within the other, that come from the puzzling East, however many you discover there is always one more; and her sweet mocking mouth had one kiss on it that Wendy could never get, though there it was, perfectly conspicuous in the right-hand corner.

VOCABULARY QUEST

Highlight and define one interesting or unfamiliar word.

Use a dictionary to explore the meaning of the word.

1._____

_____

CLASSICAL COPYWORK

Copy two paragraphs from any book by this author

Title: _____

Author: _____

Time and Place of Publishing: _____

Names & descriptions of characters:

_____
_____
_____
_____
_____

Copy two paragraphs here:

_____
_____
_____
_____
_____
_____
_____
_____
_____
_____
_____
_____
_____
_____
_____
_____
_____
_____
_____
_____
_____
_____

CREATE AN ILLUSTRATION

Make sure your artwork reflects the situation
in the selection of literature you use for your copywork.

WHAT CAN YOU LEARN ABOUT THE PAST FROM THIS STORY?

29. THE SECRET GARDEN

Genre: Children's Novel

Author: Frances Hodgson Burnett.

Published: 1911 (in its entirety)

Frances Eliza Hodgson Burnett (November 24, 1849 – October 29, 1924) was an English-American novelist and playwright. She is best known for the three children's novels *Little Lord Fauntleroy*, *A Little Princess*, and *The Secret Garden*.

The Secret Garden is now one of Burnett's most popular novels and is considered to be a classic of English children's literature. Several stage and film adaptations have been produced.

CHAPTER 27 - IN THE GARDEN

In each century since the beginning of the world wonderful things have been discovered. In the last century more amazing things were found out than in any century before. In this new century hundreds of things still more astounding will be brought to light. At first people refuse to believe that a strange new thing can be done, then they begin to hope it can be done, then they see it can be done—then it is done and all the world wonders why it was not done centuries ago. One of the new things people began to find out in the last century was that thoughts—just mere thoughts—are as powerful as electric batteries—as good for one as sunlight is, or as bad for one as poison. To let a sad thought or a bad one get into your mind is as dangerous as letting a scarlet fever germ get into your body. If you let it stay there after it has got in you may never get over it as long as you live.

VOCABULARY QUEST
Highlight and define three interesting or unfamiliar words.
Use a dictionary to explore the meaning of each word.

1. _____

_____

2. _____

_____

3. _____

_____

CLASSICAL COPYWORK

Copy two paragraphs from any book by this author

Title: _____

Author: _____

Time and Place of Publishing: _____

Names & descriptions of characters:

_____
_____
_____
_____
_____
_____

Copy two paragraphs here:

_____
_____
_____
_____
_____
_____
_____
_____
_____
_____
_____
_____
_____
_____
_____
_____
_____
_____
_____

CREATE AN ILLUSTRATION

Make sure your artwork reflects the situation
in the selection of literature you use for your copywork.

WHAT CAN YOU LEARN ABOUT THE PAST FROM THIS STORY?

30. THE LOST WORLD

Genre: Fantasy Novel

Author: Sir Arthur Conan Doyle

Published: 1912

Sir Arthur Ignatius Conan Doyle (May 22, 1859 – July 7, 1930) was a British physician and prolific writer whose works include fantasy and science fiction, detectives stories, plays, romances, poetry, non-fiction, and historical novels.

Conan Doyle is most noted for creating the fictional detective Sherlock Holmes and writing stories about him which are generally considered milestones in the field of crime fiction.

He is also known for writing the fictional adventures of a second character he invented, Professor Challenger. The author's most notable works are *Stories of Sherlock Holmes* and *The Lost World*.

CHAPTER 13: A SIGHT I SHALL NEVER FORGET

It was an awesome thing to sleep in that ill-fated camp; and yet it was even more unnerving to do so in the jungle. One or the other it must be. Prudence, on the one hand, warned me that I should remain on guard, but exhausted Nature, on the other, declared that I should do nothing of the kind. I climbed up onto a limb of the great gingko tree, but there was no secure perch on its rounded surface, and I should certainly have fallen off and broken my neck the moment I began to doze. I got down, therefore, and pondered over what I should do. Finally, I closed the door of the zareba, lit three separate fires in a triangle, and having eaten a hearty supper dropped off into a profound sleep, from which I had a strange and most welcome awakening. In the early morning, just as day was breaking, a hand was laid upon my arm, and starting up, with all my nerves in a tingle and my hand feeling for a rifle, I gave a cry of joy as in the cold gray light I saw Lord John Roxton kneeling beside me.

VOCABULARY QUEST

Highlight and define two interesting or unfamiliar words.

Use a dictionary to explore the meaning of each word.

1._____

_____

2._____

_____

CLASSICAL COPYWORK

Copy two paragraphs from any book by this author

Title: _____

Author: _____

Time and Place of Publishing: _____

Names & descriptions of characters:

_____
_____
_____
_____
_____

Copy two paragraphs here:

_____
_____
_____
_____
_____
_____
_____
_____
_____
_____
_____
_____
_____
_____
_____
_____
_____
_____
_____
_____
_____

CREATE AN ILLUSTRATION

Make sure your artwork reflects the situation
in the selection of literature you use for your copywork.

WHAT CAN YOU LEARN ABOUT THE PAST FROM THIS STORY?

SKETCHES AND DRAWINGS

SKETCHES AND DRAWINGS

SKETCHES AND DRAWINGS

SKETCHES AND DRAWINGS

SKETCHES AND DRAWINGS

SKETCHES AND DRAWINGS

SKETCHES AND DRAWINGS

SKETCHES AND DRAWINGS

SKETCHES AND DRAWINGS

NOTES

NOTES

NOTES

NOTES

NOTES

NOTES

MY LIST OF BOOKS USED WITH THIS WORKBOOK:

_____

_____

_____

_____

_____

_____

_____

_____

_____

_____

_____

_____

_____

_____

_____

_____

_____

_____

_____

_____

_____

_____

_____

_____

_____

_____

_____

_____

MY LIST OF FILMS USED WITH THIS WORKBOOK:

_____

_____

_____

_____

_____

_____

_____

_____

_____

_____

_____

_____

_____

_____

_____

_____

_____

_____

_____

_____

_____

_____

_____

_____

MY LIST OF WEBSITES
USED WITH THIS WORKBOOK:

_____

_____

_____

_____

_____

_____

_____

_____

_____

_____

_____

_____

_____

_____

_____

_____

_____

_____

_____

_____

_____

_____

_____

_____

_____

_____

_____

CLASSICAL LITERATURE CHECK LIST

__ 1. Robinson Crusoe By Daniel Defoe

__ 2. Gulliver's Travels By Jonathan Swift

__ 3. Pride and Prejudice By Jane Austen

__ 4. Emma By Jane Austen

__ 5. Ivanhoe By Sir Walter Scott

__ 6. The Pickwick Papers By Charles Dickens

__ 7. Oliver Twist By Charles Dickens

__ 8. A Christmas Carol By Charles Dickens

__ 9. Jane Eyre By Charlotte Brontë

__ 10. Wuthering Heights By Emily Brontë

__ 11. The Children of the New Forest By Frederick Marryat

__ 12. David Copperfield By Charles Dickens

__ 13. Alice In World By Lewis Carroll

__ 14. Through The Looking Glass By Lewis Carroll

__ 15. Treasure Island By Robert Louis Stevenson

__ 16. Strange Case of Dr Jekyll and Mr Hyde By Robert Louis Stevenson

__ 17. Three Men In A Boat By Jerome K. Jerome

__ 18. The Sign of the Four

__ 19. The Picture of Dorian Gray By Oscar Wilde

__ 20. The Jungle Book By Rudyard Kipling

__ 21. The Prisoner of Zenda By Anthony Hope

__ 22. The Time Machine By H. G. Wells

__ 23. The War Of The Worlds By H. G. Wells

__ 24. Moonfleet By J. Meade Falkner

__ 25. Kim By Rudyard Kipling

__ 26. The Hound of the Baskervilles By Sir Arthur Conan Doyle

__ 27. The Scarlet Pimpernel By Emma Orczy

__ 28. Peter Pan By J. M. Barrie

__ 29. The Secret Garden By Frances Hodgson Burnett

__ 30. The Lost World By Sir Arthur Conan Doyle

Made in the USA
Middletown, DE
28 July 2024

58053531R00080